The Little Spokane

Rome —
this has to
do with
where I've been

Love Gramps

the Little Spokane

poems by

Tom I. Davis

LOST HORSE PRESS
Spokane, Washington
2000

First Edition

Cover Photo by Tom I. Davis
Design by Christine Holbert

Library of Congress Cataloging In Publication Data
The Little Spokane: poems/by Tom I. Davis.
Spokane, Washington: Lost Horse Press, 2000.
p. cm.
PS3554.A937834L58 2000
811'.6—dc21
ISBN: 0966861272   (paper)
Little Spokane River (Washington) — Poetry.
Washington (State) — Poetry.
Northwest, Pacific — Poetry.
Rivers — Poetry.
Alaska — Poetry.
00-027713

CONTENTS

Dedicated to the memory of
Joseph Petta and James J. Snider

THE LITTLE SPOKANE

The naught lying before
naught is the creature
of water sighing
and whimpering:
lassitude our goddess.

Long toes with tendril
roots creep yellow iris
upstream beyond Elk
from Nine Mile:
listen to their sweet
tapering sigh.

People live auspiciously
just back from the river
but miss the point:
there is this jest
water makes
moving.

SIMPLY PUT

People are the land.
Not cross-patches,
nor fence-row, clean
or weedy, edged
around with Russian
Olive in Kittitas Valley,
ridged by piled rock
in Lincoln County; but
the land rearing up
to caress or pierce
the sky: depths, heights
declivity into water or
gulch around Vantage,
monadnock buttes
in the Palouse, granite
remnant islands among
the wheat, loess blown
east from Prosser where
Horseheaven Hills wear
green suede in spring rain.

CHILDHOOD RESOLVE

Early in The War in Valley, Wash.,
Hilton, my cousin, bombed my roadway
from the sand bank above with a stone
large enough to demolish it and
the middle finger of my good right hand.

The same one for which my father's
stories included having had the best
curve ball in Ketchikan in 1927. His finger
which of course he never gave
had a normal 90 degree bend at the first
knuckle; but my gnarled middle-finger
I give all the time. George Newell, I think,

taught me the finger when I was seven,
or so, summer, outward leaning brown
garage door, knowledge for a new world.
I knew then what I know now concerning
my good right hand and its crooked, but
erect, ugly and indomitable, middle finger.

INLAND EMPIRE JACKS

An old fact is with our 22's oiled and cleaned
we shot anything that moved: crows, magpies,
hawks, rats, gophers, swallows, sparrows, robins.
There were no coyotes or we would have gladly
shot them. Some shot old dogs abandoned Todd
out there in the ROZA irrigation project where
jackrabbits by the ton up and took stock ears
aloft, knew the shuddered shock of pellets
through the brain. Anything that moved

especially these rascally jacks that bounded
about through the sagebrush. We'd straddle
the headlight of Johnny's Model A fender
holding a 12 gauge at ready or a borrowed
22 repeater. Blam, Blam. Caught stock still
in the Model A's jiggling light, see us shoot,
fire the 12 gauge, blast splattered blood
far into mud. Jerking slowed twitching
in the rumble seat not to see their dead
still chattering eyes in the morning light
a prank piled on the principal's lawn
the color of sagebrush, dried blood.

THE A'S TO Z'S

There was only one girl
in a class of twenty three,
chemistry or maybe physics,
taught by Robert Donnelly.
She left the room to get a drink
at eleven twenty seven when
Pink cut cheese, a ripping fart
that seared our ears and split
some jeans and stopped Donnelly
mid-phrase. The only time he
paused in two whole years.

His daily lesson he wound around
the way he wound his key chain;
then he would let them spin, wind
them again like a snake coiling,
that he must have seen in the great
South Pacific War that thinned him
down to 124 and stunk his breath
and gave him that oblique, distant
stare as he would speak on in language
of chemistreze, the periodical chart,

The A's to Z's. A cloud of gas rose
where that kid sat, his feet on the seat
in front. Donnelly thought *what am I
to think of that?* She opened the door,
heard us laugh and laughed, too,
to see us laugh, we laughed more
in sheer glee, even Donnelly.

THE COLUMNAR BASALT OF MOSES COULEE

The fine grained igneous rocks grew triclinic.
One hundred foot columns, owning stupendous,
upright and overwhelming, hurtled down debris.
Sharp fragments heaped in sloped scree. Lava
extruded and flowed north and west, miles

deep, reversed magnetic iron, a lodestone, purged
crystalline reddish browns in the torrid desert heat.
We shared the magnitude, lava flow upon lava
flow, some in columns, some in pillows or billows,
time and movement frozen, pillars of drabness,

except for masses of yellow and red and turquoise
mosses like some oriental matting or medieval maps
of just dreamed peninsulas or isthmuses bridging
ocher continents lapped by seas silkier than ice.
Cut loose we drifted in a tropical island breeze.

LIVE AND LEARN,
A FROSH AT WSC

She was not shy in the CUB,
in the elevator going up. I
never saw her before, and after
I never saw her again. She
knew what she wanted and
how. I knew where we could
do it and when. We made
a plan and kept it. I led her up
the wooden fire ladder, through
a window on a dark Sunday.
In the empty dorm built for GI
bills, on a bare bunk, we did it
for a while and climbed down.
My mind blown away, an echo
purled deep within today.

GRANDVIEW, WA

We are of a place where good things come
from someplace other. All the tall young
men, all the pretty young women, all
the hard young people have gone away.

We're good if we believe we came from
someplace other. But come with me, I'll show
you where a willow-full of quail still flock
just down the hill from Judd's where water

from the slaughter house bubbles the rocks
with suds. Milk and honey from our cows
and bees spring full and we brew
such wine, we believe in joy. Spring brings

a wealth of color: apple, cherry, peach and plum.
Before bloom, calm round trees cause exultation,
sense of being where one belongs. Oh, not here,
not for us. Look, look, look for someplace other.

UNDER THE AUSPICES OF ADULTS

Some girls, scented and sweating,
bloomed round the hall. Redeemed
at a dollar and a half a plate, we
baited each other by the water fountain
and spilled over into the night.
Mel Krouse led the band and played
the sax. Wrestling coach Coke
McConnell, who also taught Spanish,
chaperoned where it wasn't needed.

Some freshmen broke some street lights
between Avenue H and Downtown.
My old man worried about the car,
while her old man, worried, worried
about his daughter while we worried
each other for fear I'd do what we'd
worried about for more than a year
parked on the ditch bank off Cherry Lane.

OUR CONCERN FOR MOSES LAKE GARBAGE, 1964

Remember when they always rented houses
with only one can and nights he'd think
of going over across town and stealing another.

One can was not nearly enough for what
they threw away, but two wouldn't be either.

He's the one who always carries out the
garbage and resents these little chores
about as much as he resents any of it.

Dogs are chained. Wind spreads the garbage.

To the north, behind the lilac, next to the garage
the neighbor built, of first grade knotless spruce,
a setup for his cans glistening in Basin summer noon.

The truck, massive door groaning inward,
crushes everyone's refuse. The operator waits.

In those days it was glass gallon jugs for wine
and cider and orange juice. The jugs and jars
for mayonnaise and peanut butter shattered.

The tough old garbage man began
to whistle when he swung the can
with loveliness and precision.
The other steps up and slaps her into first
while the one who drove before heaves it onto the lip.

The summer before, on the way to the little store,
he helped a can too quick onto that lip, dumped
before the great curved door swung back out.
The tough old garbage man said *Here, let me
get it*, as coffee grounds, wet paper bags, clinkers,
corn and corned beef cans hit the pavement.

He remembers thinning apples in Harkemah's
breathless orchard, breathing DDT after the war,
as the white garbage truck rumbled in the alley.

THUNDER DIES TO OBLIVION

Meadow lark snatches the middle barbed wire. Sings.
Sun sets. Rank weeds and ranker grass grab my pants.
Splash across a yard-wide brook, tangle succulent
watercress, charge up a blank loam bank that cows
have shredded to pale dust. Alkaline crystals
powder in clouds about my feet. Meadow lark
clips the day into pieces, interstices, somewhat like joy.

Sky layers in dust turned pink along the Cascades,
a deep blue line of casual summer, streams of magenta
smoke from fires above Rimrock Lake, stubs of charred
bunch grass like heads rise out of the burned pasture.
Perched on a wire strung across an agate sky, a warbler
clears the air, crumbles thunder beyond Ahatanum Ridge.

1944

I traded a leather basketball
swiped from Central School
for a dad-made sub-machine gun
painted black. I actually

triggered Japs about the yard
with disregard for corn or squash
and saved the town daily so bad
some girl I thought went to

drown herself in Irrigation Ditch
Number Two, the one that runs
through West Side Park, because
Jap fire-balloons burned Oregon

woods. We fought our war everywhere,
hid in the brush by the Yakima River,
wondered unflinching what to do,
had a circle jerk cause we didn't know.

THE ETHICAL THING TO DO IN THE YAKIMA

Quite suddenly after the big war
heaters in spacious Chevys, Fords,
and Plymouths gave kissing avail-
ability, vocabularized lip-lock.
Orgasm became a secret ecstasy,
released the spirit

of all the flatland girls.
In a hurry, some nights,
we'd park in a cold orchard,
exhaust reaching the bare branches
or in the vacant lot where ditches
met beneath cottonwoods.

Sometimes we'd hit the brake pedal
and red light would sheen the night,
but we wouldn't stop. We'd rather,
if we had time, head for a hill,
come up for air out of all that
touched matter, all that breathing,

all that real ecstasy becoming
ferocious performance art.
Lips throbbing we gape
at the dark valley sprinkled
with starlight, dive back into
that sea we spring from.

INDIAN POEM

This reeling Indian stalking me had this
look I turn from, but this time I said *have this*
and slipped him a buck, then dove in
to drink in the girls of the Ridge Tavern.

He trailed me. A little startled by his *Hi-ee,*
pardner, by God, now, if you gotta another
buck, I got me a jug. OK? I gave him a five.
How's that? By, God, now, forget it, I blurted.

There was no doubt with his *You betcha,*
by God, now. I'll see you around.
It's what those Indians always said
By God, now. A stillness filled The Ridge.

No pool ball clack, no juke box wail, as we all
watched him go, a head taller than anyone,
his hand he carried in a cast, in front of him
like a club. Then things got back to normal.

BY GOD, A GREAT DAY BY HANGMAN CREEK

These colors heal: sky blue, ash green,
gold yellow, silver yarrow, balsam root:
the color of their leaves green—a salty
copper—ragweed, sagebrush,
desert shadows in June. My nose drips.
I snuff it up, spit onto the red ant hill
beside Hangman Creek. Goldenrod.
Some of these stink: tansy, ragwort,
wormwood. Asthma? Breathe
determinedly from a stiffened center,
pray the diaphragm out and in.
Nature is on top in this. These colors
heal. Sniff. I am going to decongest.
But let me remind you, if it is this
world, it is mosquitoes, no-see-ums,
chiggers, slugs, horsefly, housefly,
deer fly, yellow-jacket nagging flesh.
Ant struggles out from my spit,
breathes easy, at least. I choke
back at Hangman Creek.

YOU'RE RIGHT, W.C.W., RALEIGH WAS RIGHT

> We cannot go to the country
> for the country can bring us no peace
> —W.C. Williams

"OK, I'll be country, a bumpkin in nature
to know the truth of self and man."
He took a shack, a crapper by the frigid brook.
Thought, *this is dandy, if Smoky bangs*
no closer than that corrugated can he raids.
But he was bombed, bugged, plagued
by a horde of bitter ants and pesky bees,
no-see-ums around the sweatband of his cap,
hatches of slick-winged water-pests, wasps,
besides slugs (ach), all sorts of spiders,
deer flies, horseflies, bluebottle
and houseflies that rattled against the screen
caught frantic between quick-closed glass
and mesh. Then, oh God, there was Smoky,
frightfully un-cute, in the kitchen, roaring down
final strips of bacon, dessert to two pounds
of peanut butter opened spinning, honey can
licked clean, a tin of blackberries suffered for,
vanished. Not only not funny, this guy was

no bear-man nor bugs-buzzing man.
He packed for home where neighborhood
violence is rumor between sirens that yowl.
Just relax, everything is under control.

I BLESS YOU AND SEND YOU FORTH IN PEACE

Say, there are three women, a mother,
a daughter, and wife, all in one;
or different women, a sister,
a daughter-in-law, and a best friend,
I bless them and send them forth in peace.

If there is a group of people all with blue eyes,
I praise them. I remark on their eyes and exclaim
your eyes are the blue gates of heaven.
The man at the bar with the empty beer glass,
specked from foam, is not sleeping. His
dark eyes are black like the breath of God.

I remark on the color of the skin of people.
I am of these dark skinned people: two
women with brown skin pass me
on the freeway to Bellingham.
I watch as they go by, first in the mirror,
then I look directly toward them. They do
not look at me. I would wave to them
because I love their blackish skin. Such
skin is downright remarkable.

My skin is whitish. It is the color of paste.
It is cardboard-colored. Its blemishes
are red. They are angry, but I praise even
my so-called white skin. As far as I can tell,
I am one with all The Skins. The thin, wet skin
of my dog's black nose. All the abandoned
skins of snakes and toads that are or ever
have been. I am one with them, even
leprous skin or cancerous skin. I wish
to bless them and their skin, for it is
hide to my best self. But you know

I am not flames licking the pot. I am not
steam erasing the horizon's view, nor
soft lamenting music of a wave-lapped
shore. I am less than a tornado. I am
less than ice, less than time. I have
suffered bone bruise, blistered heels,
slivers impossible to extract, cuts, scrapes,
contusions, hickeys, impossible to tell.

I am of the skin of the instep of the shoe
salesman at the Downtown Bon. I am
of the skin of the shoe of the man addressing

the Foreign Legion in the home town
in the novel being written by the friend
of the girl leaving work at five in all the towns
in Washington State, the skin of her hand
groping in her purse for keys to her Volvo,
the skin of the purse, same as the man
who made the keys and named the car.

If I would, I could be a vast vagina. I would
take into me all the elements. As they enter
me gently, I will their tenderness, the soft,
pliable substances of lithium and Valium,
the resilience of iron, copper, manganese,
the gold, archaic ritual of starling's wings.
Carbon, oh, carbon, is there a spirit released
when you burn? Oh, to let enter the gross
ivory of frozen mammals, great lords of jungles
with their mammoth tusks, walruses, seals,
whales stranded on beaches in Oregon.

I would open to all of these if I were the skin
of a vast vagina. Or what about a whole
bunch of sperm or how about just one
great big one as big or bigger than all matter

or space or even time. This is easy to say;
but I'd be space to accept the sperm
of ease and peace to plant in the egg
of trust and grace to grow such harmony
of courage and toil, I'd build a being
both male and female, a hair on his ass
and a fulsome grin in her cranium.
Hey, hey, well-a-day, love the splendor.

SONGS OF ROCK

My rock emits sound,
crystal teeth gnashing,
a deep voice stone denies.
My rock emits sound.
These rocks so soon extruded
crystallize into dark columns
algae highlight. We've watched
the sun across the basalt,
heard talus singing.
These rocks are words. Word
is rock, my habitation. Older
than this are spirit in the rock:
cornerstone, keystone, heartstone.

RECOLLECTION

Bruce told me about how he
and his father, my Great Uncle Irv,
visited up to Elk on Otter Creek
and my dad, who was just a boy,
went out to catch dinner. Fifty
rainbow! Otter Creek is pretty
much dried up now. Fishing
for Protestants was a religion
in western towns. An enigmatic
strike to the tip of a bamboo wand
considered God to be flesh; wriggling,
lavish, stippled-sided, fried golden,
plead God's-luck transcends fate.

PUTTING IT MILDLY

These are the bleak facts:
The world we have,
the bald planet of the future
purged of oppression,
by scorching winds
off the desert.
We shall overcome
say the small,
the creatures of lightness
and some sweet smell.

BOXING AT WSC, 1954

Gordy Gladson, four time National
Collegiate Champion, grew up brawling
swabbys from Bremerton Navy Base.
Nose flattened beneath thickened eyebrows,
at twenty-four he carried a punchy demeanor.
Hung from sloping shoulders, his arms seemed
to reach his knees. Sparring with him the first time,
he whipped the snot out of me. I woke up
four hours later, doing my sociology.
When we touched gloves, I whispered,
so Coach Deeter wouldn't hear, *the next time,*
don't hit me so hard.
He said, *you hit me hard, first.*

After winning a football game, male students
drunk from vodka laced oranges and watermelons,
flasks of bourbon chug-a-lugged, fiends not fans,
roared out of the stands, the entire field tilted
and rolled as pent up frustration diffused. Hundreds
rocked the goal post pipe until the upright broke
and dropped directly onto his head. Watching
from the grandstand, I wasn't surprised at all
that he never staggered one little bit. Gordy Gladson.

MY DA'

He nailed the plywood square to the telephone pole
at the edge of the yard. I threw at the red circle
to learn control—one ball over and over all summer—
to be as good a pitcher as he, the fastest ball
ever seen in Ketchikan. In the one game I pitched,
ninth grade against eighth, I pitched fourteen walks,
with only one strike. Cliff McGhan kindly swung at three
bad pitches, and Coach Coke McConnell yanked me.
Though I hit a crisp triple, I never pitched again.
Though I hung out a smart ass in right field,
my sophomore year, a jester, in practice, I never
knew the silent joy of catching flies or pitching
strikes on a baseball team. As a junior, I began
to win the mile in the Valley, when I was the only
one who ran around those irrigation ditch
soft meanderings before just any old fool ran.
Skinny legs, slow beating heart, capacious lungs,
lonely running was easy. Back away from the track,
he would maybe never cheer because I didn't run
dashes, because I did not dare pitch again,
with this ordinary, *you can kiss my ass*, attitude.

ABOUT MA'S JULY 5 BIRTHDAY ON MOTHER'S DAY

Mom, these days spring cloys, repose
slackens, the intermediate state of being
—summer by July—begs the question,
Why was I born? I say again, if it had not
been for you, I would not be. Now or July.

Later, lying beside the Little Spokane in wild
alfalfa beginning to bloom
its lavender heads shaking in the light,
brilliant even above the river's roar.

The thought of you, your ice blue eyes,
a private longing to have known you
forever, alfalfa around my mind, I lie down,
open-eyed with the cool May sky.

OFTEN IN THE BLUE MOON TAVERN

in memory of Richard Hugo

Stan Iverson bellowed *You Motherfucker*
as I'd swing into The Moon on my way
somewhere else. His skinny whiplash
Montana attitude, a glint of mica
in the true vein of his granite congeniality,
a reality about who and what I was

round about then. *Motherfucker* he roared
again, the four syllables rising up his
growling timbre to hold the last rich R
sound, the R the way we out West learned.
And, oh, I was, I was what he
accused. I diddled hi diddled, indeed I did.

My old friend, Stan Iverson, did not shirk
but made me pay. I declare, these years
later, with the meagre patriotic zeal I muster,
the only other thing I am, with this gritty
growl of an R, God forgive me, a flag waving
and burning motherfucking American.

MAN USES GROCERY CART AS WALKER

The sort of June afternoon eternity was thought up,
a large pink man hangs onto a nicked and rusted cart
appropriated from the neighborhood store.
To the store and home, he leans on the cart for balance,
wheels stall crosswise in the pitted asphalt, jerk loose,
and wobble him up the middle of the street, gallon
of paisano asleep on a blue shirt in the cart's basket.
An American man, on his left foot a blue plush slipper
drags under at the heel and the black wingtip wags
its tongue as he drags his swollen right foot to keep it on.
The buckle on his belt is broken. He stops to pull up
his pants. He is swollen and pink. His white hair was
once orange (that kind of man), skin, where unfreckled,
pink. He struggles to keep his pants up with legs apart.
To hold the cart takes both hands. He stops, looks about.
In the little store the girl is kind, has known him since
a child. She looks to her shelves as his pants drop
when he struggles for change. His grey cotton trousers
fall to his heavy thigh. What hangs from broken
underwear is youthful, enshrouded with hair on fire.
We are frightened for him. He reaches up, stretches
fingers into the flecked blue sky, cries *godamn it.*

RIVER

Rivers I own:
Yakima, Spokane,
Okanogan, Wenatchee, Little Spokane,
Klickitat, Little Klickitat, Satus,
Colville, Bumping, Naches, American:

owe their rapture to me,
that industrious riot that eats the land,
turns to ruin mountains,
will not be stymied, will eat away
all we own, possess us with a spell,
enchantment of water sings
our bright love awake, tense
disorder, water on a rampage,

Skagit, Nooksack, Cowlitz,
Cascade, Suiattle, Sauk,
Stillaguamish, Duwamish, Nisqually,
Skykomish, Snohomish, Snoqualamie,
Humptulips, Wishkah, Wynoochie,
Quinalt, Elwha, Queets.

LOGGERS AT THE SUNBURST TAVERN

Big guy shoves over his meat hook with fat sausage fingers.
M'names Mike. Smoked granny glasses. He may be tame.
He smiles, but it may be a snarl. Whatever, it is best to be
friendly. I am friendly.

The little guy tilts up his jaw, the prow of a tugboat
fringed with pink Christmas trees. He bristles,
not just from the bush. *Name's John, call me Rabbit,
I'm a McCullogh, m'self.*

*Thinned three hundred acres without a hitch. Huskys,
now them suckers, the chain'll fly off cutting brush
and knock the gas tank loose. Now, them McCulloghs,
gotta go in full throttle.*

His approach to life is chainsaw. He straddles emotions
with a highly lubed, hardened steel edge orbiting
through wood. Mike says, *Yep, I'm a McCullogh, m'self.
No use for a fuckin' Husky.*

His thighs in overalls are phone poles; trunk, if timber
would make a timber man quake. The entire tavern
resides in the lenses of his dark glasses, gives a man
pause. My head a tiny dot.

I gotta little McCullogh in the trunk of that Impala out back,
has a thirty six inch bar. That sucker'll even cut them boxcars
lengthwise, lengthwise 'longside them tracks like a banana,
cars, ties, bed, the works.

Never miss a stroke. His voice rumbles but is calm, he crosses
his hands, leans back. Sunburst slows, a kind of country
silence, at last, as of long summer afternoons back home,
sunshine in an open door.

The little cat, Rabbit, is up. *I'd limb a grizzly.*
Eyes glazed and raged, *damn near did. This griz*
comes into camp, clumb up on his hind legs like this.
Raises up, grizzly growls.

Sunburst quakes like woods at dusk. He manifests
a chainsaw in his upraised hands. Pulls the cord,
engine roars. *You bet your sweet ass, turned that sucker*
like a chipmunk. Sheeeit.

That little redheaded man stance, love me, love my kids,
otherwise, rip and tear, motherfucker, rip and roar. *I'da*
trimmed 'im, too, before he'd flinched, just like a chipmunk,
I'm a McCullogh, m'self.

MOOTSY'S: THE STATE OF THE UNION

A woman—drunk—from Lame Deer, Montana
sat to the bar, leaned onto Betty
while Betty explained how her dad taught her
to love everyone. All of Betty's teeth,
upper and lower, are missing in the middle.

At Mootsy's, Noel leans way across the bar,
speaks in the voice my ancestors chose.
This Irish accent is not bland. His head
weaves in rhythm to confidence he shares
concerning Serbs, mystic rhomboids of land,
thriving trees, the border lands among the Rockies,
the stretches across the territories Canadians
become Canadians in. These tough old sons of bitches
in Dillon and Libby. Montanans and Idahoans don't
need fudge. His hands never cease talking,
tracing the webs of words into kinship-saying.

At the pub I think of grapes,
early green drops of promised elixir,
their prolixity dangles modifiers
with a sweet, fulsome flavor.

I would tell anyone how my Great Aunt Fay
taught me to pluck roses with my thumbnail
for vases all spring and summer into fall,
taught the tight reigns of love, how unpicked
they stop blooming. Plucker, pruner, no weeder.

One young guy went to pick up his kid.
His ex-wife was gone with the kid and
all the six thousand dollars
worth of new furniture gone.
The guy she'd shacked up with
from Montana gone.

We don't much believe in stupidity
but this one flu-eyed guy leans to his left elbow
and sort of jauntily with his soft square mug
lectures me on racism:
She's a racist just because she thinks I hate her
stupid ass when I wouldn't care if she died.

Two big black guys sit at the bar. One's feet
sit flat on the floor my feet don't even reach.
Harold's at the other end of the bar where he
always sits. Some other guy I don't know stares

into his schooner. Free peanuts and dollar beer
for Tuesday. Sounds are muted and joyful
between songs, country and blues. *Hey, Rick,*
give these five guys a beer. How the Ethiopian
who whispers furtively to no one on his left
came to be in Spokane wearing a Notre Dame cap
is anyone's guess. Rick says *My friend, Tom,*
here, bought you five guys a beer. One of the guys
with his feet on the floor says *Well, now, I thank you,*
I come from Baltimore. Now, I am here.
We raise our glasses in toast, even the Ethiopian.

When Noel speaks English
the Irishness of his IRA past
condenses speech into seventy
languages of nods, blinks, growls,
and grunts that say *my nose*
flattened at the bridge means
character. Since he's broken
from the past, if you hire him
to paint your house, you may
breath easy treading water.

Rick's dad's Samoyed
chewed the tail light off
his '57 Coupe De Ville
and shit pieces of red
plastic for three days.

Harold fought Golden Gloves to Chicago
'49 and '50. We celebrate 62 years together.
He works anyone into the ground. His lame
wiry six feet looks able to spar me into the wind.
The mummy hand-wraps, teeth guard in place,
smell of sweaty leather gloves, sopping wet
sweat suit, checking punches with elbows,
deep respect, a kind of love; this is boxing.

A young guy just off the bus from Virginia
takes ticket-tab after ticket. Five dollars,
ten dollars, twenty dollars, another five,
opens them, wins a dollar, two dollars,
opens, nothing, nothing, nothing,
for the Walkman he'd planned.

ANACORTES, EAST OF FATE

Broad Commercial Avenue, better known as P Street,
slopes north, downhill to saltwater, Alaskaward,
where the men who don't come back have gone to.
Boats, narrow shapes on water, widen water's dilemma,
the going out onto it; and boats broaden Anacortes' streets.
Like the compass needle, boats always lean north,
where they go when they go back. Here, in Spokane,
rough guys, bearded, with peculiar hats, shirts buttoned
to the top, looking beyond, sitting on benches
within earshot of the great falls, maybe, this far inland,
only these guys—drunks or panhandlers—know about fish.

Why they go North is one thing, but what keeps them
there? The challenge is fish. Taking salmon in purse seine,
where water swirls and eddies, rip corks to the bottom,
puke back up, boats flounder on reefs, or sink dead out.
Or King Crab, level the saltwater tanks so the boat
loaded with two ton traps won't list, take the young men
down for a measly profit, stripped of meat, bones in deep
water slime. Toss those bones, read the future. Fishermen
weather inward, salt breezes diminish. Water stacked
by tide and current, brutal wind, we are less than jade

water cliffs. Water is bigger than us. Hearts of mothers,

of sons, lost fishing the lean North. Daughters, whose mates,

victims to fish and crab, hold the long wish sound,

Eskimo-style, air hissing, *sshhhh*, when they say *fish*.

WHAT I SEE TODAY

Springer spaniel Winston sniffs around the pickup,
through the marigolds. He sits to scratch his left ear
with his right rear leg. Circling the compost, he smells it all.
He limps on his left leg, injured courting a cross-island bitch,
kicked, I think, by a jealous and irate owner. Too much
dignity for a dog. I can yell at him. He will cower.
Cower dog. I will yell it next chance I get. *Down,* I will yell.
Dammit, Get down. I'll hit his nose, smash his thick
neck with my fist. He won't go down. His front legs
refuse to bend. With all my weight I push down. His legs
buckle. His lucid caramel eyes full of wonder do not cower,
do not doubt my authority. *What is his great strength,*
he asks. *How can this man muscle me down, make me
remain prone?* His thick legs lift his muscular body
inches off the rug. *Stay,* I scream. *Damn you, stay!* I blast
him a good one to the top of his beautiful white and liver
head. Winston doesn't flinch, turns his dignified face up,
lies down. He lives for me, loves my act. Thinks me big man.
I know better. This springer deserves better. This bird dog
deserves, what, pheasant under glass? This hunter has
earned meat, heart, steaming hot guts. This springer
will not eat ice cream, oatmeal, nor his own puke.

SKAGIT VALLEY

Across his coffee
he observed her cross
the lounge. She was

squeezed. The bulges
of her ornamented
his ache. Her credentials

read Phi Beta English
Department Blue.
His love of language

meant tongue in her
cheek. Chaucer knew.
Donne said do it.

Her lips leapt out.
Her hair wasn't done
but did it. Such nice

stuff. In those taut parts
English Departments

miss the point.

He thought,

Me, too,

I'll learn at the fount.

AMEN, BROTHER, AMEN

What if amens after prayers, legions moan Sunday,
mean something, not agonized emulation of evil
pained in bones of wretchedness. We have no comfort,
for no one dares mourn, for rain melts salt.

Look up and think *rain*; soft summer raindrop
evaporates as the next lands near it. What if amens
were horizons, parched and rock-strewn, grayed
by streams of sagebrush and up behind, north
and east, pine and fir gentle the shoulders
into meadows brisked by red blueberry brush.
Amens after prayer.

BEING DANGEROUS ALASKA STYLE, FOR A
SPOKANE NATIVE

Port means drunk in Alaska. The deep red drink speaks
Angel in Tlingkit, spells disaster thirty foot waves tinker with.
Going north for crab or fish, boats season at bars where justice
resides in the face of raw egg. *Whosoever's kid that is sure*
looks like Diedrickson. Where the hell is Diedrickson, anyway?
Port or something guzzles up drizzle in evergreens that clamber
up mountains inland till there's no earth for them just rock and ice
that never melts. On shore, the crews or men known as the boats
they came in on—Randy Lady rubs against Northern Mist—
bunch around who has some pot and where to smoke it and when.
Natives are drunk on something. They don't show it. Engineers
drink alone—whisky—or with someone from town they've never
known. Someone who won't go out on boats, won't even eat fish.
Engineers keep boats afloat, listen to the skipper's stories.
The only one to unwrap the boy caught in the web, dragged
overboard, dragged around the drum. Skipper on the radio.
Drowned. Wyz-chip-now-ski. Yah. Dragged around the drum.
We're on our way in. 10-4. James Wyz-chip-now-ski,
that's how you say it. Here's how you spell it . . .
The crew sits rapt in the galley; James wrapped in his sleeping
bag in his bunk. Skipper at the wheel for once studies the water.

Engineer straddles the bilge, painted green each winter, moves
slightly with the roll of the boat, stares at the giant diesel, painted
black and red. *Easy to work on*, about all he'll say. His head poked
out, his shoulders up around the gray ball cap, is why the crew
name him The Heron. He comes back season after season,
straddles the bilge glistening newly green, stares at the engine,
intent on the minutest detail. He hums a sound he doesn't hear
above the roar the engine adds to the sound of water
outside the hull, moves with the pitch and yaw. Wind tears
the surface of the water lifted up and across the twenty foot wave
in slanting light irradiated jade green two thousand miles south.
Billows up. Blasts the crests off. The boat angles southwest,
into the trough, a ten hour run. No talk for once. No tall tales.
Back in the bar there's humor. Imagine long swells, eight dolphin
diving to the flank, tide ripping the seine straight down, fish
bright and silvery in the boat's belly. Alone at the bar's end,
The Heron stares into the mirror. The natives are drunk
on something. They never show it. Not much.

ROZENCRANZ, THE RED DOG, AT RIVER WALK

The miracle of a detached separate thing, a dog.
No name could be worthy: Rosauer's for just how
much that big dog ate, Rollerblade for his smoothness,
Rosie for the color of his nose and the name
of Big Mike's big black Lab, and finally, Rozencranz
for Heron's favorite movie. This animal ennobled
life where he ranged Ash Street down Water Avenue,
up Main; a horse and artillery, he owned where he peed.
Sebastian says, *With a pink butthole just the size*
of his rose of a nose. One day Rosie bit what he should
not chew, the butt of the man whose Mastiff shredded
his tongue clear through. Too much dog for town,
out to Tolstoy Commune with him. Runs deer, coyotes,
and for the pure dog joy of it, now. Still cottonwoods
stir without the least breeze and the water-tumbles stir
a melodic roar without an act of will. Still I sit looking
beneath a July blue and wonder at the weather. How
just now the honey locusts serpentine through all
these greens: absinthe, aquamarine, avocado,
emerald, reseda, I swear. Rozencranz's two-toned
coat blended with rye grass heads, yellow pine bark,
last year's honey locust pods, unnamed reddish

and yellowing browns, was one with all the pedigree
only Raymond Hardesty claimed: Red Wolf, Airdale,
Malamute, Australian Shepherd. This gorgeous dog
strolled into and became the browns among greens:
lime, minty, parrot, malachite, sea green, shamrock,
teal, turquoise, tourmaline, verdigris, veridian,
If this dog didn't lead me into paradise, what was it?

NUSHAGAK, UGASHIK, PORT MOLLER, EGEGICK, NORTH NAKNEK, PORT HAYDEN

for Miles Johns

Good old Cliff Johnson knows two types of joke,
        the Texas or the Brown Bear,
The *give me liberty or give me death* joke —
        a vague rasping of voices out of sync
or reality. Texans will not eat you
        and your shoes up. Brownie mauls
to make palatable what's left of Texans
        or what there's no name for, Alaskans.
Even the kids on the porch of Cliff's Bar
        speak bear talk, bitten short
words, diced and cut by months of storm
        Asia did not want, like duck brains gone
bad, heard in shrill winds, to holler bear away.
        Dream is ugly hibernation cage.
These towns lean from Brown Bear; lonely
        leans, wind wracked bone chill.
Nice people, whites, skippers and such
        come by boat, do not like Cliff's. Natives
right, whites should not go there. Where
        every night we watched the girl

who could not stop dancing in fright,

        the pool-shooting Eskimo master shot,

who never aimed, dared anything, a kid who

        hated his father he never knew,

rumor he couldn't forget, Mom choking

        on a bottle in her throat. The view

out the window, my favorite panorama

        across the rutted gravel street

by the Russian Orthodox Church, chipped

        paint and rusty bruises, four

power wagons, winches, cable and all taking

        on color of dead gray dirt, a '56

Studebaker station wagon, rear door jammed

        down like mine used to be, two

retired 6 x 6's, choked snowmobiles in grass

        higher than shattered eyes, fuselage,

bent frame and all, of a biplane, ripped aluminum,

        of someone's dream of a way out of here.

THE RHINO TAVERN

Black street under black sky, not a light anywhere
but the streaked rainwet pavement with shimmering
red or green or desolate streetlight gray. A night
to be out alone looking for a hunker down beer,
a soulful time, a longed-for conversation into what
and when. But, by the way the handsome bartender
handed the guy in the softball suit four quarters
for music, I knew this wasn't the place to get in from
the cheerless night out. Where had I driven?
I didn't know. Home, somewhere I couldn't go.
Refuge? Rain in rivulets the wipers didn't sweep
away. Rhino Tavern flickered in the gloom, a mood
to scavenge any pleasure. A loft to the left, I go up
to take in the empty scene below. By the juke box,
the ball player says to the air, *I played number 34 because*
I played tonight at least. Nearby bartender and another
handsome guy lean across the bar to each other.
Blonde guys. The girl comes up the half log steps,
corn-tassel hair, freckles, but she is not friendly; goes
to get my Bud and hot dog. Ball player leans his back
to the bar. Across his shirt, black letters spell *Rhinos.*
His handlebar moustache appears glued on. I look hard,

trying to figure it out. Are these guys assholes, or what?
The blonde guys repudiate the ball player with his sad
face. His pants are tight across his big butt; I wonder how
he can run at all. The yellow pine table varithaned like
the half log steps and the peeled log railings are
a snare or maize, that old honky hippy country flavor
that doesn't roost here anymore. This is the sort
of into I'm out of; we all are. She's back with my dog.
She's pissed but not at me. Pale green relish, pale pink
wiennie hangs out of limp damp bun. I'll eat this dog,
drink this chill beer. Get the hell home, out of here.

COMMUNITY EDUCATION TRAINING AGENCY

Cracking the footrest against my shin, John's
auto-wracked body wrenched his wheelchair
maliciously if he thought you were in the way,
twisting his huge body to glare peripherally
with one good eye. We would drive to Sedro
Wooley, picking up the twisted sisters, one
head the shape of a sweet potato, the other
softball-sized, with big eyes, glassy as polluted water.
This job converted me listening to so-called
Christian radio, the only talk shows on in '74.
CETA, a program for the sly destruction life-
depleted compassion with Marilyn's cerebral
palsy-wrenched body, a taut stagger on her
knotted tippy toes, reeled unassisted
from the yellow Dutch Reform farmhouse,
chipper as a gold finch: CETA had no name for *assisted*,
back then. Back then, two brothers whose bulging
Pekingese eyes belayed each other's dread, having
thrown their brother into a roofless well out by Lake
Sammamish, sat together in the back, side by side.
Shoulder to shoulder, all day, a shrill soundless cry.
No plan or theory, I read *Winesburg, Ohio*

and *Canterbury Tales* two times: the boy
whose moan ceased only when I read, whose head
was a tall silo with desolate blues at the bottom
that never blinked, the 38 year old Downs woman
never out of the house till that year, the Downs
man wisecracked his only words, *No way, Jose,*
over and over, and Louis Pigg, poor boy, they
and all the others listened, and some understood.
Louis Pigg's body spoiled by a doting mother
who never exercised him, demanded nothing,
bony legs wrenched from sockets at hips, knees
and ankles, shoulders horribly hunched, elbows
and wrists and fingers all pulled and yanked
without surcease, crooked spine, twisted mind,
all the pain of angry muscles displaced, poor boy.
The first day, the day the women workers hired
me, I had to help him pee because he couldn't
reach his man sized penis. My job, to take it out,
aim it, shake it, and put it back. So, the first day,
the day the women hired me, I unzipped his
fly and out plopped, sticking straight out, curved
up, this big old hard on. Shocked, no, more than
that, horrified. What was I supposed to do, his
pleading eyes in that muscle-wrenched face said,

Please release me, let me go. I said, No, no.
In fear, I grew angry for him to let it go. He peed.
I zipped it back, hot as a curling iron, speechless,
stepped back to glare. His eyes soft as spring
dew, rimmed with tears, lonely, he sang, for good
God's sake, he sang in this voice agony gave him,
Hear that lonely whipperwill, he sounds
too blue to fly, he sang, for God's sake, he sang
The midnight train is whining low, oh, sweet
Jesus, instead of thinking of beating him up,
I'm so lonesome I could cry, I should have just
beat him off. I handed the job back to the women.